Joe an

alw[...] cherished
friendship

Aryeh

The Soft of Pisces

THE SOFT OF PISCES

Poems by

Allen Dale

Exposition Press Hicksville, New York

First Edition

ISBN 0-682-48875-5

Printed in the United States of America

To my Yon
and
to all of my blood

Contents

The Soft of Pisces

Yes, I Do—Yes, I Will

Clammy hands, wrinkled brow
    starry eyes
    and
    mind cluttered with thoughts of
    a lifetime gone by
    and
    of one to come.

What is right?
I crave my bloodlines
    as
    I crave my love.

Starting all anew,
    is it fair to a few
    who will depend on me?

An angel came to me
    but a few months ago
    with flaxen hair
    and soft eyes of blue.

She said—
    I've been searching for you
    a lifetime,
    and now I've found
    a warmth as mine to share
    as one
    forever and a day.

The time finally came.
Swiftly the hours ticked by.
Why am I chosen?
What can I offer?
Who am I?

The angel finally came again
    with outstretched arms
    softly touching with
    hands like mine
    and reassuring me that
    she picked me over all.

How lucky to be one in two,
    glued arm in arm,
    floating down the aisle
    with music playing softly
    (I know not what),
    strangers' eyes watching.

I searched them all but
    saw nothing but my thoughts.

Quietly my words spoke out
    until a mere whisper left
    from lips
    uttering silent sounds
    and
    there she was again
    calm
    soft-spoken and beautiful.

I thought
    she sounds just like me
    and

she does
and is
for
I do
and
I will
'til
evermore.

Hello, World

I'm sorry—I have a vice.
By today's standards . . .
    it's being nice.

I Know You!

How proud and lucky I am to be a Pisces.
Yes, you Libras, Virgos, Cancers, Gemini,
    Aries, and Sagittarians,
    I am always one up on you,
    for . . . I know all about you.
You, Aquarians, are close to me, yet far away.
And all the rest of you,
    together with the others,
    can never know . . . or . . . understand
    the total me—
For I'm a part of each one of you, and you do not
    even suspect.

I possess the strength of the bull, the quickness
of mind of Gemini, the justice of Libra,
together with strong points from all of you . . .
mellowed with my own.
Oh, yes, I'm unique . . .
for I love you all as
I love myself.

Thank You for You

Give us this day to touch
with softness—warmth—and
love so much.

Exciting moments to cherish
of yesterday and now—
I've searched a lifetime
and finally found.
I wonder why and how.

As you say—God has blessed us,
for
I've always taken and now I give.

You've taught me togetherness . . .
faith and trust . . .
and . . . how to live.

The softness of your smile will keep me
longing forever
and awhile.

Found

Searching like your sea gull . . .
Questioning . . .
        until I stopped beside you and
        with the softness of your voice
        I gained trust and love and
        stood beside you and let you touch.

I See with My Heart

I did not see the sun directly
        but I felt its beauty
Glistening on the trees
                in the forest
                        near where I live
I did not see the rain
        but the reflection of its tears is
Cleansing on the brush
                in the forest
                        near where I live
I did not see the hummingbird
        feeding near me
        but I sensed its happiness
                in the forest
                        near where I live
I do not see my Father when
        He walks beside me
        but I know He's there
                in the forest
                        near where I live
For you see with your eyes
And
I see with my heart
You see—I am blind.

Strength

I love a smile that . . .
        loves to love,
        a warmth that's warm.

I love a laugh that gives.

I think of you each passing hour,
The one that smiles and laughs
        and . . . strengthens me with the will to live.

"Good-Bye"

Few times in our life we are blessed
    with meeting a stranger—
        to chat with
            and listen to—and
                    becoming friends . . .

For in a flicker of time
We are separated—perhaps
            forever
                but
That brief moment will linger on
In our hearts . . .

                    for
The love and friendship we experienced
Was a gift from Heaven
To cherish
                    in our mellow moods.

I Would if I Only Had the Time

Will you love me as you love
Your children?
I would love you as I love mine
I would
If I only had the time.

Will you come with me and live
The simple life?
I would come with you
I would
If I only had the time.

Will you forget the loves all past?
I would forget all of mine
I would
If I only had the time.

Will you live for me and me alone?
I would live for only you
I would
If I only had the time.

It's You

It's you—it's you, it's you in my heart
each minute, every hour of the day.
It's you—it's you, it's you that I love
forever, forever and a day.
It's you that I live for . . .
It's you that I wait for . . .

It's you that I pray for, every night when I'm away.
For I know when I see you,
Yes, I know when I see you
    that you'll love me even more than yesterday.

Your touch—your touch, your touch is so touching
    in my dreams the whole night through.
Your love—your love, your love is so loving
    when I am feeling blue.
It's you that I'd die for . . .
It's you that I'll stay for . . .
It's you that I crave for, each moment, every minute
    of the day . . .
Forgetting all the troubles,
Forgetting yesterday—and living altogether for today.

Quiet Love

Listen to the quietness of the wind . . .
    the softness of the rain.
Listen to my eyes . . .
    when they speak to you.
I feel home when I'm with you,
Lost . . . when you're away.
I've known no greater love
    nor . . . will I ever.

The thought of your love when you are with me
    will keep me warm on cold nights and
    dreamy days.
Yes, I've loved you.
I love you now
    and
    I always will.

Happy

I love you
    to love me
    to love you.
I love to see you
    to see me
    as I am.
I love the warmth
    you give me to give you
    each day
    each hour
    whenever you can.
Your touch is my touch;
    your mouth belongs to me.
My thoughts are your thoughts
    which no one else can see.
I'm happy.
I love.

Remembering

The warmth of your hand
. . . the softness of your smile
. . . and the sweetness of your mouth
. . . will keep me longing forever
. . . and awhile.

Anyone You Know?

Are their closets all that clean
    that they are unable to see the good
    in the bad?
Have they never had . . . so much as
    a bad thought, knowing that
    this is judged equal to an evil deed?
Unreal . . . so perfect in their own eyes,
    yet they have not lived.
And who are they to criticize?
Have they ever known want
    or . . . never known greed?
Indeed!
Do you see warmth in their eyes
    when they smile . . . or
    are they cold like their snow-capped teeth?
How friendly they may seem,
    but . . . all along they put you down.
I hope for them that . . . they see the light
    someday . . . before time runs out . . .
    like me.

Close

We differ so slightly.
I am me—
    you are you.
I am yours—
    you are mine.
You love me much—
    I love you more.
I kiss your lips—
    you kiss my mouth.
I hold your head—
    you hold my hands.
We touch.

When the Wind Dies Down

I watched the trees in the breeze—
    the solid oak with little sway,
    body still, yet
    flicking its leaves,
    letting you know it's listening, then
    quiet again
    when the wind dies down.
The willow with its branches low
    looking beaten as it touches ground
    so deceiving—looking frail, but
    only bending . . .
    so smart and coy
    as it stands erect again, unbroken
    when the wind dies down.

The Sabal palm waving its fans:
Look! Look at me!
Look up!
Here I am—
I'm speaking for a change and
tired of being calm, but
I'll have to be myself again
when the wind dies down.

Lonely

I feel home when I'm with you . . .
Lost . . .
when you're away.

A Dream Warm

Such a warmth to see this stranger
in the midst—
a crowd so huge, but yet
she stands tall . . . and graceful.

Her flowered dress draped so completely
within the realms
of pants suits and slacks . . .

So petrifying . . . and beautiful—
My eyes were searching . . .
wondering.

Will she never see them?

Alas . . . finally . . .
    and the gaze became an eternity
    of excitement.
Thoughts flashed
    and
    my stare softened with her smile.

Can she really be so warm
    and friendly . . .
    and honest . . .
    and . . .
Can she . . . like me?

I Know You Two!

You are my mirror
    and
I see the reflection is good,
    for
I love me
    as never before.

Love's Freedom

My love, I saw your sea gull today
and . . .
you are right.
The freedom it enjoys
is heavenly to watch.
It glides freely, unmolested . . . unquestioned,
and . . .
in its own way . . .
cries out,
friendly but searching . . .

Confident and beautiful,
yet . . .
it has an inward quiet of peace and tranquillity.

It is questioning until
it stops beside me
and . .
with the softness of my voice
it gains trust and love
and . . .
stands besides me and
lets me touch.

Deep

I sit here in the warmth of the sun . . .
thinking of warmth elsewhere . . .
alone . . .
wondering.

Swift Days

I woke up today to the summertime of my life,
When only yesterday it was spring.
I look forward to today,
        yet . . .
        wonder what wintertime will bring.

Clean

I have always been breathless
        when walking and searching
                the forests and meadows,
Watching in amazement and
Listening to the stillness of such
                        unbelievable greatness
        which none of us could create.

I've always recognized the supreme
                        artistry
And marveled at the sight
But
Recently I witnessed it at even
                        greater length,
For
                I gave up smoking.

Too Young to Know

Son—we're going to the Courthouse today.
Your new daddy wants to give you his name,
OK?

You see—your father left
        and doesn't mind at all.

Brother and I stood tall
        before the big man in the large room.

"Boys, do you accept your new name today?"
Yes.
"That's all."

Next week I brought a note to school—
The announcement came as quite a shock.

All my friends asked how to spell it then—
I didn't know—they laughed.

You see
        I was only ten.

Insight

Let your Christmastime love of God
        shine through your eyes
        each day of the year.
And let the gaze reach and touch upon
        all you may see.

Jay Bird

How graceful and beautiful you are
Winging through the air,
Your brightness always shining,
Inquisitive eyes sharply searching.

Chest out . . . strutting proudly . . . watching . . .
Flitting so busily . . . then sitting,
Asking question after question
With only eyes to speak.

Always answered . . . not always understood.

Dreamy to hold . . . so soft,
Like peaches,
        and warm . . .
        like first love.

For Jay Bird is not a bird at all . . .

Jay Bird is my son.

Riches

The largest gift of all is giving of ourselves,
        and
The amount of giving will be your measure of love.

Proud

My son didn't play football—
    Dad did.
My son didn't play basketball—
    Dad did.
My son didn't play in band—
    Dad did.
My son wasn't a school wheel—
    Dad was.

But, what my son is—
    Dad isn't.

Game Time

The band, playing their wild music,
    while boys and girls are playing games . . .
Strange . . .
The games so different now from when
    I was a boy.

The dudes all looking alike, molded . . .
    mustache . . . long hair . . . tight shirts . . .
    chests out.

Are there no individuals left?

Shallow eyes looking straight ahead . . .
    and right . . . and left . . .
    but turned inwardly only on themselves.

How great if their souls would do the same;
    then, perhaps true love would be theirs.

A happy throng . . . I doubt.
Briefly, perhaps . . . but then
    there is tomorrow.

Worry

Have you ever wondered about
. . . your one and only true love
. . . when she continually takes
. . . birth control pills
. . . when all you do is touch
    and . . .
. . . she dates only you and
. . . only friends . . . but not very much?

Hometown

One of many cities in today's world
    where the girls are healthy
    and smiling
    with no tranquilizers necessary
    and
    where the men are listless
    and dragging,
    taking physicals quarterly
    for reassurance.

Chance

Each day of our lives
God gives us
    an opportunity
    to greet Him through
    a stranger . . .
    an opportunity to greet he
    or she
    with love from our soul
    and
    respect from our heart.

Whether the stranger be
    down and out
    or
    on a pinnacle of refinement . . .
God has given life to all
    on an equal basis.

Love has many depths.
Who are we to know that
    some stranger, sometime,
    may need you as a friend
    and, perhaps . . .
    you may need him.

A Duet of Forgiving

Can you forgive me,
Or are you unforgiving like I used
to be?
Can you receive me in your arms
again?
Will you believe the loving words
I speak to you when
lights are dim?

Will you forgive me?
I don't know why I did the things I
did
to hurt you so;
I only know
I've come back to all the things I
valued so very long ago.

Please forgive me . . .
Give me one last chance to be your
man to you and
Give me back the tenderness I gave
to you
So very long ago, for
I love you so—yes
I still love you so.

Yes, I'll forgive you;
I want you back again just
like you used to be . . .
Yes, I forgive you;
I want your arms around me
holding tight
With soft loving words throughout
the night,

Like we used to do . . .
Yes, I forgive you,
          for I love you so.

I've always taken,
          now I give;
You've taught me faith and trust
                    and
          how to live . . .
Yes, I forgive you;
          I forgive you
                    for
I love you so . . .
          Yes,
          I still love you so.